T0147001

HER *Heart*

Won't He Do It

KISHA GREENHOW

BALBOA
PRESS

A DIVISION OF HAY HOUSE

Balboa Press books may be ordered through booksellers or by contacting:

Balboa Press
A Division of Hay House
1663 Liberty Drive
Bloomington, IN 47403
www.balboapress.com
1 (877) 407-4847

Because of the dynamic nature of the Internet, any web addresses or
links contained in this book may have changed since publication and
may no longer be valid. The views expressed in this work are solely those
of the author and do not necessarily reflect the views of the publisher,
and the publisher hereby disclaims any responsibility for them.

The author of this book does not dispense medical advice or prescribe
the use of any technique as a form of treatment for physical, emotional,
or medical problems without the advice of a physician, either directly
or indirectly. The intent of the author is only to offer information
of a general nature to help you in your quest for emotional and
spiritual well-being. In the event you use any of the information in
this book for yourself, which is your constitutional right, the author
and the publisher assume no responsibility for your actions.

Print information available on the last page.

ISBN: 978-1-9822-1479-1 (sc)
ISBN: 978-1-9822-1485-2 (e)

Balboa Press rev. date: 10/25/2018

My Princess…..

It's okay to cry, I see how hard you try to handle your heart, and I know you want to live a life without heartaches or pain. I'm asking you to take a step closer to me when you hurt, let me heal you. Remember my chosen, King David. He cried out to me in his fears, disappointments, and sin, and I answered. You are also my chosen one, and you are my daughter… So, it's okay to cry. I don't expect you to pretend that pain is not real. It is truth and tears that will give you the freedom that I want you to know. Now, let go of that part of your heart that only I can heal. Let your heavenly daddy hold you while you cry…

Love,
Your King who Wipes away your Tears
pinterest

Contents

INTRODUCTION

In life you will make decisions, some decisions will be amazing and bring you much joy. While others you will want to request a "Do Over". However, some decisions will require that you learn to live with regret!

Lord I pray that I shall decrease so that you may increase O'Lord. I seek your approachable spirit and your humble ways. Please provide my family the peace and understanding that passeth all understanding. I'm here Lord, Send Me!

Kisha Greenhow

That's My Dream Girl

I was Born Lakisha Morrison, June 23, 1975 in Columbus, Ohio. My mother raised me as a single parent until third grade. However, my grandmother had ten children and I never noticed a difference, I always felt wanted and loved. Holidays and cookouts took place at my grandparents home where I spent a-lot of my days. And I'm thankful for that! I was never dropped off at a stranger's home and never had a babysitter. I had a REAL grandmother.

My Uncle Tarrent served as every bodies daddy. I

think we all have that one person that handles business and sets everything straight. Well, our family was really never the same after my uncle Tarrent died in December of 1992 and my grandfather would pass five years later in 1997. Real quick rundown of my family: Uncle Junior loved music and would take you to see two movies in one day. Aunt Neil purchased me dresses with bells and is full of wisdom, Aunt Kim the artist who loved to make me cry when she talked about my forehead. Until I overheard her tell my uncle why. " Its big and she needs to be prepared for when they talk about her forehead." It worked I was totally desensitized by the time i went to school. My uncle Fret loved his cake. Aunt Shon was more like my sister she was the youngest and we were only four years apart. We even later married brothers. Aunt Diane yea that's my girl, 4'11 can hold her liquor and talks ahole lot of split. My Aunt Deborah wow beautiful light, loves hard and pure. She took care of my Uncle Tarrent without a second thought. If we never truly expressed how beautiful that love was, thank you and we appreciate everything that you did!!! My Uncle Patrick Died at the age of 12 when he fell out the window. The death of Patrick brought my grandfather to Columbus, Ohio. and he and my grandmother reconciled. My mom, she is so special. Like for real she is really special. I know that God really has mercy and grace on her life and it has spilled over onto my sister and I. God has that resurrecting power over her life.

My Step-father Ronald Hill provided that stability and security that only a man can do. Even tho he was not my biological father as I grew older I loved him more and more. Although the relationship between he and my mother later ended I believe my freshman year in college. I appreciated everything that he did for me. He provided for me and he did not have to…

Once my mother married my Stepfather our location changed. I went from an all black school to being the only black girl in my grade level. There was one black teacher in the building and guess who got her. Yep,and she was tight.! She moved in the middle of the year her husband got a new job. She showed pictures of her home, I remember seeing an inside pool. Her name was Mrs. Ellis and she taught at Ennis Elementary school in Whitehall, Ohio. Mrs. Ellis checked me real quick. My zip code had changed but I had not yet caught on to the cultural difference. Education was a priority and learning was key to a good life. I went to not having any assemblies and never knowing who made honor roll. To attending all assemblies and 75% of the class making honor roll. One day I received a really low score on an assignment, and I was laughing. Mrs. Ellis said, "What's funny? Have you looked around to see where you are and how well everyone else is performing. Well, Let's just say that was the day my life on learning changed. She is opened my eyes, and now I can see! That next year I made honor roll and was student of the month. I had faithful teachers who provided extra support to me during lunch and recess. So, I believe in the power of Great teachers who are changing lives one student at a time.

Our family was so large the cookouts were like family reunions and picking numbers for Christmas became necessary for gift exchanges. Running around at grandma's in the basement, eating my cousin's candy and then tatling. I was coined the Termed Ronaberet from Mrs. Pat, because I told everything from the weather to who was seeing whom. But my fondest memory was that of my grandmother reading her bible and my mother taking me to church even before I understood. My mother spoke of my self esteem and I contribute that to God's hand on me from the womb. However, I also poked my chest out due to my grandfather. I walked by my grandfather while on the porch talking to his friend Mr. Booker. As I walked by to enter the house I overheard him say, "that's my dream girl right there". Girl, drop the mic I was no more good! That would be all the validation I would need to gird my spirit, letting me know that I was worthy to be loved and to be loved with all your heart and soul.

Yes, so the power behind that head snap was power! The Warriorett Drill Team filled my life and direction with discipline, character, and value. Our Advisor was Allison Leadbetter mow Mrs. Copeland, who was just a baby herself. But she made a-lot of women by nature into ladies, and we thank you!

DISAPPOINTMENTS, WILL EXPOSE YOUR BROKEN PIECES

What do you do when you save yourself for that one person and they never see you, or your needs. Was I asking too much? Was I not being appreciative of what I had? I learned a-lot about my needs as a women through my disappointments. I'm extremely loyal to a fault and I believe in family and building a legacy. I yearned for something authentic. My understanding was if I was willing to go all out for you, you would move heaven and earth for me. I learned that I truly loved the Lord and that he loved me.

I expressed on multiple occasions that if you truly have any issues with me, take it to God, and he would speak to my spirit. Whenever I attempted to try the spirit by the spirit, I never received an answer of confirmation on my marriage. However, our family grew and we continued to hustle and prosper, or so I thought. I later understood our foundation was not built on solid ground and before long it would fall. (Mark 3:25) If a house is divided against itself, that house cannot stand.

It's important to capture your true essence as a child. It's important you know who You are before you step foot into this world. This world is vicious and full of evil vile spirits. You need to know that you are beautiful, kind, courageous, loved, and God worthy to accomplish his will. You also need to know that you will make mistakes and that life will not always go your way. That will not mean that you are not able to be a used servant of God. (Proverbs 24:16-18) for a just man falleth seven times and rise up again but the wicked shall fall into mischief. The enemy is a liar and will replay all your faults in your mind over and over again until you believe it! Stop, because those that are evil, never think they are evil. Fall forward and allow God to heal those broken pieces, and allow the test to become your testimony.

I remember being 25 and putting our kids to bed reading my bible walking the floors anointing doors and kids head with oil. How did I know to do this, I don't know!

I vividly remember reading in my T.D. Jakes Bible purchased by my mother-In-Law a story about Sarah and Rehab. It explained how the Lord judged Sarah and Rehab both the same. Now I was totally confused, like Sarah was pure and Rehab was a prostitute what foolishness is this. This really upset me like: this women of ill repore is being judged the same as Sarah. Well, that was when I was 23-25 I later learned to call it the "Now or Later" stages of growth. Some have the courtesy to learn these lessons privately, while others business is displayed on Channel 12 and Radio One.

Nothing better than a scandal with patty perfect, It hurt and it was hard to accept at times, (Psalm 119:71) states, "It was good for me to be afflicted, that I may learn thy statues." When God allowed me to be afflicted he allowed me to see that you walk upright not by your sight but by faith. You are genuine not by your will but thy will." So, pretty much the Lord showed me that as I saw myself in Sarah, I was only a season away from being Rehab. When I learned this spirit of humility, my guards dropped, my ego was twisted, and my faith in God was tested. My humility was developed by God for God. During this point in my life I had three children all under the age of 5years old. I came home from teaching to take care of the kids 100%. I received a call from a college friend Lisa.. We had been communicating by phone for months. Discussing family life, old times, and life after college. Then one day the phone rings, I pick up and she reads a bible verse to me! Then proceeds to explain how her marriage and home fell apart and how she wanted to cleanse herself. The only problem is I was left holding a bag with none of my belongings inside. I now understand there are some things you need to take to God and leave them on the altar. As I look back God was exposing things that I was praying about. During this time my maturity level was still being developed. I appreciated everything I had, but I never thought anything about it. I was too busy working for it. This was the beginning of my eyes being open to the evils in life. I found myself in the pouring down rain with no umbrella, Or so I thought.

The day before mother's day I'm at the kitchen table with the kids cutting cheese and lettuce for the tacos I was cooking. My husband walks in and says we're going to my mothers for Mother's Day. I said, "No, I don't want to visit your mother for my mother's day. This was the beginning of me speaking up for what I wanted. I was told how disrespectful I was. This was one of the worst moments in our marriage. Once again my prayers were beginning to expose the questions within my prayers life. We were both in our twenties, from single families and without any blueprint of how to deal with the trials of life. We went from being best friends working towards our dreams to these broken pieces, we had no clue of how to put things back together. At this time I was 26 and just a little girl myself. I now had three children all under 5, stay at home mom, and we were in the middle of opening a business. So, what do I do, I proceed with life, never healing the broken pieces. At this time I became a walking zombie, full of emotions and no understanding. I remember the pain and the emotions being so unbearable that I just wanted it to end. I just wanted the pain to go away.

I wish I could say that my prayer life intensified and that I selectively changed my circle, my husband got saved and we lived happily ever after. Nope, this was only the beginning. "You never came to save me you let me stand alone. Out in the Wilderness alone in the cold. I found no magic potion, no horse, with wings to fly, I found the poison apple, my destiny to die." No Fairytales, Anita Baker

I don't want to make any excuses about what took place next so I'll state the facts.

On August 11, 2003, I went to my room called a college friend that I began talking to Back in June.

When he picked up the phone I straight out said, "can we have ***" He Made arrangements to see me and so did I. Now, if you know anything about the two of us. This was so out of character. This was the first time we were ever together. During college we went to dinner and even stayed the night with each other, and nothing happened. The act sedated the pain for a while, but once the thrill wore off. I had a new issue on top of the pain, and its name was guilt. I would return a few more times to quench my thirst, but my thirst was never quenched. Now, I was in pain due to betrayal and disappointment and the fact that I had put my hands in it. By placing my hands it in, I had just made a huge mess, and it was about to get messier.

Just as I leave teaching night school my husband calls. "KISHA, everything else is a blurr. He was aware of what had taken place and he was furious. To be honest I think he was more embarrassed. In a previous conversation we had discussed the possibility and he was stunned however, he fully acknowledge that in order for me to go there, I was hurt, not only hurt but devastated. Now, this reaction he was having now was totally different. As if it was different now that others were aware. We worked on our marriage through prayer, and dancing from the ceiling sex. However, all this went out the window soon as the school year started back in August. I could not believe it, I was feeling so secure in our marriage, I was happy. He never acknowledged any wrong doing. This hurt me to my heart, and not only did he never acknowledge anything he began to use it to his advantage. The pain was back and so was the thirst. However, I knew that I would leave before I ever disrespected myself again. He used my moment of weakness to control and manipulate me, while he continued to do what he had always done.

So, an already ugly situation just became even uglier, and had flipped from him to I. He would now use me as his source of bitterness for years to come. And I took on the guilt and wore the shame for years, as he continued to do what he had always done...

So, my broken pieces were never healed, yet In return I was being blamed for everyone else's brokenness. Wow, just the thought of another being so dishonest. That Eleven day journey had just turned into 40 years. Now, one thing I'll tell you is that I always had a project in progress. I was raising our three children by day, working out at the gym, and editing the paperwork of our future business by night. We had to fully have the group home furnished from day one. I had my office all decorated from things I had gotten from my mom's home. My title was the Admissions Director. However, once the doors open, I had no title, I had no office, I was not involved at all. I remember the day of open house, I was so shocked with disbelieve I did not know how to stand up for myself. Because I did not understand how someone could feel right about totally excluding me out. I later learned that he explained it to others that we made an agreement. No, that was not my wish, I had worked and the deal was to help him start his and we would start mine. That never happened, and each time I tried to start my own it was knocked down. The marriage was getting worse so after Christmas I started substituting at a local middle school. Fulfilled my teaching requirements and enrolled at the University of Cincinnati. Im telling you, I was always hustlin doing something, time was never wasted.

During that same time I was visiting local theology schools. Yes, I'm Jonah and the more I grew and developed I often wondered had I caused this storm with my disobedience on so many levels. See I wanted God to come into my mess and fix it, but he said NO, I'm not coming into that mess you have created. But I'm ready if you're ready to go. I take responsibility for my part! It would be ten more years before I officially surrender 100% and walk away from that life to live God's will. Three teenage children, lived in a half million dollar home, practically a stay at home mother, teacher turned business owner.

No money saved, savings went into starting my business. It was a risk but faith filled decision. We were separated just five years earlier for three years, and upon his return things were worse. It was here that I learned about legions and strongholds. If the issues were not healed prior to the separation then upon returning things would be worse, for legions would raise up. (Luke 8:30) Jesus asked him, "What is your name?" "Legion" he replied. The storms were raging and like Jonah on July 11, 2016 I asked God if you get me out of this I will not look back! My time had expired and Jesus wanted my all today? No, more excuses...Get in Now!

This is when I learned how much in Love my father is with me. When Jesus was about to be arrested in the Garden of Gethsemeane. Peter drew his sword, to try and defend Jesus from the authorities. However, Jesus said to him "Put your sword back into place. For all who take the sword will perish by the sword. (Mathew 26:52-54) So when you're tempted to seek revenge remember this. Do you think that "I cannot appeal to my father, and he will at once send me more than twelve legions of angels? (Mathew 26:53) Now, that's gangsta! What a mighty God we serve...

Place your Order Please

Life becomes difficult to maintain order. I don't think we ever thought to reorganize our schedule. It worked well in college, however, we then added child number one, marriage, house, child number two, child number three, a business, and built a new house. All from our college mindset and organization. Wow, I just answered my own question, we never reorganized. Order is important for one's spiritual health, marriage, family, and household. Each day we walk outside our homes we encounter different spirits on our jobs, friends, organizations, etc. And multiply that by the number of folks within your home. If your home is clean and spotless when you leave and someone invades it. You're likely to notice that which is out of place. However, if it's a HOT mess upon you leaving, then it may be days before you notice anything is missing.

Let's start from the beginning. When I think of order, I think of oil running from the top of your head to the bottom of your feet. Think of God being the head, the torso being the man (strong arms to work), and the legs being the woman (ladies we make things move) and our goal is to have it flow to our feet (representing our children)...

(Ephesians 5:33) "Nevertheless, each one of you also must love his wife as he loves himself, and the wife must respect her husband. " The bible provides man and women each their responsibility in a relationship. If you lack respect for your husband in the beginning.

You will not grow to respect him. It should already exist in the beginning. Know what your needs are. Know one needs to know but you, so be honest with yourself when selecting a mate. Men know after the first date if they want to be with you for the rest of their life. They will love you from day one. Just because she respects you does not mean that you love her, and just because he loves you does not mean that you respect him. Ensure both are present before proceeding to offer up the gift of marriage.

Order and how it pertains to the family is the next order of business. First order make sure if you need medication do so please. Because none of what I say next matters if you are not in the right mental state. At the end of my marriage I can say had we done this we may still be married today. I look around at the families going through the same devastation of divorce. We all appear to have it all, beautiful spouses, children, college, successful careers, beautiful homes. So, what's the problem, I don't know about the others but I can sure tell you, we were out of order. During college my husband and I were best friends. We met seven days into me stepping foot onto campus. He was a senior football player, say no more right! However, he was the sweetest and treated me like a princess. My high school sweetheart was a football player. When I told my aunt she said leave him alone now, he only wants to get in your panties. I laughed, she one year later married his brother. I left this part out originally However, I have to tell it. While I was freshman I befriended another freshman and one day as he walked down the steps in the square God said, "That's your husband". This is not the man I married, Recco pursued me and we both just went with it, even tho we were complete opposites. My husband

and I hustled together from the very beginning. I walked pregnant with Keion at my graduation. Recco was already working in Amelia as a coach and AT-Risk counselor. I worked through college at a local bank which merged my senior year. After graduation I took the summer off after giving birth to Keion. That fall I was hired as a Henrico County Police Communications officer. This job allowed me to pay off credit cards and any debt either of us had. Recco held down the household bills while I saved with every intention of buying a house the next year. However, while visiting my mother it was placed in my spirit that we purchase a house soon so, I began preparing. While Recco coached I held it down with Keion, taking graduate courses at state. Working, preparing the wedding and the paperwork for purchasing our first home. All he had to do was show up and move in, we worked well together.

This same building, creating, mindset went into play 4yrs. later when we paid off all debt. I was pregnant with our third child. Putting business in order to come home and take care of our soon to be (3) children whom were all under 5yrs. Old. This was not an easy decision for me, I loved teaching, I loved my job. But I had an amazing time getting to know each one of my kids like no other. I was so very proud to have had that opportunity to stay home, Life slowed down and I enjoyed them without the hustle and bustle of outside obligations. I also was in shape because I worked out everyday, that was my break and their extracurricular activities. That stretch period when you look back was fun and brought out the best in us.

In the meantime, we continued to raise our family on a tight budget. We attended free story times at the library, we visited the gym daily, the kids had pool time, gym time and arcade time. This worked up until the middle child attended school. Every year we brought season passes to King's Dominion, free movies were shown on Wednesday at 10a.m. during the summer. Within my bag was popped popcorn from home and hug juices, lol, don't play I told you we were on a budget.

On to the next project! My husband was aware of my aspirations to own and open something. He stated, "Ok, Let's open mine then we will open yours". So, I placed my graduate degree on hold dived into the paperwork of mental health. During the day I raised kids, and after they were sleep I edited, revised, and typed policy and procedures. It would be three years before all revisions, house preparation, state inspections, and license to operate was achieved. We purchased surplus electronics and took out second mortgages and borrowed the rest from his brother. We were $100,000 in the red before we had ever made a dollar. We were young and the stresses of life were piling high. We were raising three small young children. Keeping our eyes on each other became a chore more than an escape. We were no longer Best Friends. I took for granted that he always provided, and he took for granted that I held down the fort with his children. They were my life and I would not have had it any other way. I never took breaks or asked for help, I wore this as my badge of honor. It's very important to balance family with your life. I'm thankful for my angel's Mrs. Pris and Momma Gandie I absolutely love you. These ladies filled in for my mother who lived in Ohio. But visited as often as she could and we the kids enjoyed our trips to grandma's house, loves you.

In a nutshell things began to start crumbling down because we were out of order. We stopped being each other's first love. We instead became parents and business partners. Everyone will go through things painful, hurtful, betrayals are lessons of life. Allow those lessons their proper healing time. Do not allow your rage, anger, or bitterness an opportunity to dwell with the devil. Repent, heal, and order your steps in the Lord,

Allow forgiveness to flow from your head to your feet.

I thought i was a great mom because i never took a break, but this was false. I needed a break to better care for my family. And the Lord's calling was pushed even more to the back. It's important to preserve your marriage, teaching your children how to live a balanced life, with gratitude. Place your order and change the order of your family.

You owe it to your children and your grandchildren.

When your car pulls up to McDonald's your car set's off their signal "Welcome to McDonald's how may I help you today." When you take your seat at church within the pews. The signal went off and the worship leader has requested your order. However, In order for your order to be placed you must open your mouth. How many of you are present today. However, when asked, "has the lord been good to you! Every mouth should open, every tongue shall roll. Thanking the lord for the breathe within your body. A closed mouth does not get feed. So, you can remain in line for hours but not until you open your mouth will your order be placed. We all have different tones and pitches some are high soprano, low, or deep alto. I don't really care how you order but I need you to place your order! Now, how does that order differentiate in the house of the Lord you may cry, jump, shout, run, moan, I don't care how. However, when the servant ask,"May I please take your order" every mouth should be open In the house of the Lord. He has been to Good to your spouse, children, family, church, organization, and

HE deserves all the honor and praise. Now open your mouth to be fed. Amen!!!

When you cry out to the Lord, step back and watch to see nothing but the goodness of the Lord. It's hard, I know, to sit back and watch. But let me tell you about my God.

(1 Corinthians 16:22) "Do not touch my anointed ones; do my prophet no harm."

I have seen families, relationships, people,marriages, homes, and finances rocked. The World Calls it Karma, we call it salvation. If someone were to attack one of your children, you would be ready to curse heaven and earth. Well, God feels the same way about you and I. So, please stay in order keep your tongue, mouth, actions off those who have done you wrong. Pray for them. (Mathew 5:44,45) love your enemies! And pray for those who persecute you. He causes his sun to rise on the evil and the good, and sends rain on the righteous and the unrighteous." What, think about that for a minute because I know I'm convicted. I cooked my husband a great meal, when I liked him. And I was extra nice to the kids when they did everything I asked. However, the word says the sun sets on the good and the bad and it rains on the just and the unjust. We must stop allowing our emotions to control us. The Lord is calling order and it requires discipline and consistency. As Pastor Watson says, "God's hands are bigger than ours." God will handle your enemies in a way that gets their attention. And they will know that it was I AM. So, you keep your hands off his children, pray for them right or wrong. Baby, God's got it, and he is all about justice.

A LETTER TO MY DAUGHTER / A TIE FOR MY SONS

There is nothing I'm more proud of in life than my three children. Keions' light has shined so brightly from day one. I never knew a love like this before giving birth. And with all my heart loving her, I didn't think I had room to love another. Then here comes Booger nose Charlie (Mr. Kyle) and this is the male version of Kisha. Lord he makes me love myself and dislike myself at the same time. Such a pure hearted and genuine kind person and a first class man, love you dude. Jordan, momma's baby, up until he hit puberty. I"m now like what happened to my baby. This is my hard worker, money maker, in whatever he decides to do! Love you Jethro. Let's pray for our children:

Lord I surrender, I'm just an imperfect vessel aiming to you for strength, protection, compassion, and discernment, dear Lord. You have placed these beautiful children in my care, to one day serve your kingdom and do your will. Somedays the task is so heavy for the world is troubled. Please give me the strength to do a great work and provide a model of honor, respect, and strength. Please place a hedge of protection around these children from the top of their heads to the bottom of their feet. All these blessings I pray in jesus name, Amen…

My greatest lesson to you is (Mathew 7:6) "Do not cast your pearls before swine." (Proverbs 26:11) "As a dog returns to its vomit, so a fool repeats his folly. Let us dwell on that for a moment: My daughter was presented pearls during her Sweet Sixteenth birthday. In life no matter how wonderful you are to your mother and your father, rejection is a part of life. It's not for you to hold yourself hostage to others. As if to say,"your gonna love me." (by) No, God Tells us that if we are not wanted, valued, accepted (Mathew 10:14) tells us to shake the dust off our feet, when you leave that home and town." And when you leave do not return, learn the lesson and move on. For returning is like returning to your vomit. (Proverbs 26:11) " As a dog returns to its vomit, so as a fool repeats his folly." Ladies, daughters, mothers, sisters Aunts, Nieces, I need you to see yourself as your father sees you. When Keion walked in the room her Dad's eyes looked up and the sunset. I met my earthly father for the first time Oct. 22, 2016. After speaking to him for 4yrs he believed I could walk on water, for real. However, even before I met my earthly father I always felt the love of my heavenly father. And Even tho unlike my daughter I lacked the love of my earthly father. However, I knew I was loved, adored, and that I was loved, adored and that I was special! Just as my daughter. Now, here is the lesson. Do not give dogs that what is holy; do not throw your pearls before swine. If you do, they may trample them under their feet, and then turn and tear you to pieces. Consider the habitat of the swine it dwells in mud and is recognized among all the animals as one to not devour. They are unclean. It will eat anything,even you. Pearls are found at the bottom of the sea covered by its shell and within the shell it dwells alone. It's very important that you understand how precious you are and not just in appearance but within your heart. (Proverbs 4:23) above all else guard your heart for everything you do flows from it. You will finish college, marry, have children, and above all of those you will be required to fulfill God's purpose for your life! So, your spouse, children, friends must all value and respect you and the boundaries you represent. With all diligence pray to God, before making all life altering decisions. Remain still until you hear his voice. Trust that he will give you strength to endure the yes and the no. Trust your spirit of discernment (1 Corinthians 2:15-16) The price to pay is one that goes against everything you saw in your father's eyes. That love will be replaced with hate, lies, scandal, deceit, betrayal etc. And if you go into the mud with the pig you will get dirty. The pig is fine with the dirt it resides there. However, you and your pearls which are found at the bottom of the ocean covered in its shell, all by itself. You are use to dwelling in secure, safe, loving places... From which wise discussions come. (Philippians 4:13) "I can do all things through Christ who strengthens me."

Prayer Wall

I know this may sound corny but this is what happened. My Aunt and I went to see War Room and within that week I turned my office at home into a war wall. I understood that I was under spiritual attack and that I was going to win this war in prayer. I did as the license plate had instructed, I began to fight. My prayer wall consisted of the following scriptures. I had been under attack for over 15yrs. But at the appointed time and place I aligned myself with God. And Humbly I went to the Thorne and laid at his feet open to surrender.

(Isiah 54:17)
No weapon formed against you shall prosper, and every tongue which rises against you in judgement you shall condemn. "This is the heritage of the servants of the Lord and their righteousness is from me," says, the Lord...

(Isiah 59:19)
So, as the result of the Messiah's intervention they shall reverently fear the name of the Lord from the west, and his glory from the rising of the sun. When the enemy shall come in like a flood, the spirit, of the Lord will lift up a standard against him and put him to fight. For he will come like a rushing stream which the breath of the Lord drives.

(Luke 10:49)
Behold, I give you the authority to trample on servants and scorpions and over all the power of the enemy, and nothing by any means hurt you.

(Ephesians 6:10-18)
"I believe I am free in the name of jesus the Holy spirit and God Almighty who fills my body, heart, mind, spirit, and soul... Amen.

(Deuteronomy 3:22)

You shall not fear them, for the Lord your God shall fight for you.

(Mathew 25:41)

"Then he will say to these on his left depart from me, you who are cursed into the eternal fire prepared by the devil and his angels.

(1 Samuel 2:1,10)

My heart exults in the Lord; my heart is exalted in the Lord. My mouth derides my enemies, because I rejoice in my salvation… The adversaries of the Lord shall be broken to pieces; against them he will thunder in heaven.

(Ephesians 6:12)

For we wrestle not against flesh and blood, but against principalities against powers, against ruler of the darkness of this world, against spiritual wickedness in high places.

(Psalm 61:2)

From the end of the earth will I cry unto thee, when my heart is overwhelmed: lead me to the rock that is higher than I.

(Psalm 18:6)

In my distress I called to the Lord, I cried to my God for help. From his temple he heard my voice; my cry came before him, into his ears.

Wow, I am amazed as I look back at these prayers. And understand now just how I was protected from harm, seen and unseen. (SMH) Thank you Lord, I'm so grateful because it did not have to turn out this way. I was praying for God to heal me, my home, my marriage, my family. I was looking for a powerful restoration. What I received in prayer was a powerful revelation, It's Over!

You know when it's time to go because your out of gas or you feel yourself about to slip. Well, In January of 2016 I understood I was out of gas, and it was going to cost me my life. If I did not move. I told my family, husband that was it and that I would be getting a divorce. Lots of loose ends had to come together that year. But prayer brought about a change in me and all the other times. I had said it. It was real this time….. We were each in separate bedrooms, living under the same roof, raising children.

When I look back I actually thought I was doing the right thing for the children. It's more important that you demonstrate healthy, loving, relationships for your children. Prayer is very important when making life changing decisions. It clears the lines of communication between you and the lord. Be patient and understand you are on God's time. Also, be prepared to accept when God says NO. Rejection is God's protection. When the answer is No, be wise to follow his full instructions.

Formation Please

There are times my heart is heavy and overwhelmed. However, the Lord spoke to me today, If I opened your eyes today that means I am fully prepared to take care of you! I will feed you, I will clothe you, I will protect you." (Psalm 61:2) When my heart is overwhelmed lead me to the rock which is higher than I. I praise God daily because it was not suppose to turn out this way. The Lord Jesus Christ is not a liar. Romans (6:23) the wages of sin is death. I often felt the price paid for my sins were costly, until one day the Lord showed me the possible answer choices without grace and mercy:

1. Death
2. Homelessness
3. Disease
4. Reputation

It was then that I realized that in-spite of my sin, the Lord still showed grace and mercy on my life. Because when it's all said and done "more is said than done." It could have been me outside with no food, no clothes, no friends, or just another number with a tragic end. But God! Did not see fit to let none of those things get to me. And I want to say thank you Lord for all you've done for me." I was a sophomore in college when the Lord said, " I'm still calling you". I ran not because I did not want to serve, I was not sure of what I was to do! And it was overwhelming to me living to the expectations of God not man.

It was difficult for my husband to understand, why? I had such a need to be! His wish was that I go to work raise the kids and be happy with a big house. (Esther 4:13-17) explains it best when Mordecai sent this reply to Esther. "Don't think for a moment that because you're in the palace you will escape when all other jews are killed. If you keep quiet at a time like this, deliverance and relief for the Jews will arise from some other place. But you and your relatives will die. Who knows if perhaps you were made queen for such a time as this. Go and Gather together all the Jews of Susa and fast for me. Do not eat or Drink for three days, night or day. My maids and I will do the same. And then, if though is against the. I will go in to see the King if I must die. I must die." So, Mordecai went away and did everything as Esther had ordered him."

It's important that I note that at this time Esther wept.(in the movie). Esther had to die to self for she understood this life she was given, was not her own.

I was working out at the gym with the 5:30 crew, shot out to the Ashland YMCA. When one of the Elders stopped in front of me to say, "Nice job as the Mother'sDay speaker." I said, Thank you. Mr. Young then said, "I'm just going to say one thing, then I'll leave you alone." I'm all smiles because I just know he is about to say, (something political) He then said,"You're a preacher! " I froze, and In my mind I said, "how did he see that". I worked out in a different place that day, and as soon as I started my car and started to drive down the road. I busted into tears; You remember those tears when you got a whoopin and you could not catch your breath, that cry. Once I gained control of my breathe I explained, " Lord I love you with all my heart. And I'm honored that you desire to use me, I just don't want to disappointment you!" As I write this statement, I realized that I was disappointing God, by not trusting that he knew this, and he needed me to decrease so that he might increase. So here I was in the belly of the fish, and when I'm spit out. I'm running straight to the Lord, here I am Lord... God was still there waiting for me, but he was packing his bags... lol

It was only through prayer and the preparation of fulfilling my calling that I was released from the hurt, shame, lies, pain, and misery. Humble yourself, repent,pray, and ask God for his help to ease my aching heart, ask for strength to continue to move forward. "Some people will say you brought all this on yourself." And others will say " you did not deserve this." However, the only thing I need to be concerned with is, "What did God say?" (Job 13:15) Though he slay me, yet shall I trust him. Thank you, Lord for your Grace and your mercy!!! I love you.

As I sit in the home once occupied with my husband. I'm totally aware that it was not suppose to turn out this way, Or was this all built in vain. I never went to God to ensure that this marriage could hold my purpose. And because I did not seek God I'm left to lose all these strings, to return to my first love. But this pain was avoidable had I just adhered to what God spoke into my ear some twenty years ago. Here I made soul ties where Kingdom connections were required.. I took my time cleaning each room from top to bottom. I was also cleaning my soul. Each day, week, month, "I got a little bit stronger." The songs that I cried to each time now, I can listen without shedding a tear. I went from asking God to rock me to sleep on the couch to resting in the spare bedroom. I was no longer angry, or hateful, just ready to move forward with a clean heart. The kids are getting to know their mom without the frustration and pain. And they deserve that. My son came home this week, and he just stood in front of the office and smiled. And my daughter just told me today "I'm not stuck on money or things, I just want to be happy" that blessed my soul. She was witnessing a beautiful change in me and I cried, but even as I cried, I expressed that this is what I want. It's just the process, and I'm getting a little bit stronger everyday. (John 5:8) Get up, pick up your mat and go home. (Mark 2:11) I'll tell you, get up, take your mat and go home. It was time to stop plucking around with the chickens, it was time to soar with the Eagles! No more excuses, my expiration date has come! Let's get it! Thank you Pastor Watson, such a classy man! (facebook service due to snow) The standard of Christianity is to be like Christ! Not like T.D. Jakes, Pastor Watson, not Paula White! We are to raise up the standard in our behavior, actions, and conversations. So, cut it out! That thin line gets confusing and truly overwhelms my soul. See this is why I cried, because I never wanted to disappoint the lord. I love him so, I must surrender my needs and honor his will which means, I need to talk to him daily and adhere to his word and obedience.

God is birthing a nation of women bringing restoration, reconstruction, reconciliation, reciprocity to our families, communities, schools and our nation. The lord took a rib from Adam, to create woman! To be a help meet. Well ladies it's time! That help which was established at the beginning of time. Woman to Woman, it will require a secure man of God to hold up these women, selected by God to go forward.

He wishes to use you as his vessel, so men be prepared to execute the launch. The world is filled with such evil, it is necessary to be covered. (Ephesians 6:12) I Pray that he prepared your heart and mind to pass every test of the adversary. For it is written. (Isiah 54:17) No weapon formed against you will prevail. Every tongue that shall rise against you in judgement you shall condemn. We have been playing church, but we now must be fully committed and filled with the blood of jesus runneth over. Our time has expired church with playing holy. It's not impossible to move the mountains in front of us, (James 5:16) states, the effectual fervent prayer of a righteous man availeth much.. Confess your faults one to another, and pray one for another, that he may be healed. The church is a hospital and we are sending patients home without healing. Why because our souls lack discipline. (James 4:1) resist the devil and he will flee. Required power to perform open heart surgery on the broken hearted, to release the strongman, the abused, proud, and the diseased. It's just something about that woman! (Genesis 32: 24-30) I'm not letting go til you bless me." Jacob stayed behind by himself, and a man wrestled with him until daybreak. When the man saw that he couldn't get the best of Jacob as they wrestled, he deliberately threw Jacob's hip out of joint. The man said, "Let me go;it's daybreak." Jacob said, "I'm not letting go til you bless me." The man said, "What's your name?" he answered, "Jacob". The man said,"But no longer, your name is no longer Jacob. From now it's Israel (God Wrestler). You've wrestled with God and you've come through." Jacob asked, "why do you want to know my name? And then right then and there he blessed him. Jacob named the place Peniel (God's face) because, he said. "I saw God face-to-face and lived to tell the story."

While I went through the deliverance phase. Each person I ran to, in one way or another they would forsake me It was here that I learned that God wanted me all alone at his feet. He wanted my total attention surrendered. So, that when he raised me up no one could get the glory. God wants it to be clear that it was he that kept me. And he alone! (Mathew 5:44) my father in heaven said that I shall love my enemies, and pray for those who persecute you. They are in pain and have been in pain for so long. They don't know why and refuse to accept any accountability for their life's condition. The devil has them so far gone on the other side, that they don't even know that they are on the other side. Your not hurting me. Christians are being required to raise up a standard. With all the evil in the world, we are going to stand and be the light necessary for change. And (Ephesians 4:31-32) "Get rid of all bitterness, rage, and anger, brawling and slander, along with every form of malice. Be kind and compassionate to one another, forgiving each other, just as in Christ God forgave you. Amen!"

DIMENSION ACADEMIC PERFORMANCE CENTER

When all hell is breaking loose in your life you will run to do exactly what you were required to do, serve. When I tell you I love what I do, it's real. And I know it was nothing but God because I could never have put this together. The Richmond Heat track team attended an invitational meet in 2013. While at the meet I began researching SAT and ACT curriculums. Found an excellent program and called for training dates. It was pretty expensive and it would be a year before I attended. My husband was all in and unlike before I told no one. For the next year I would research and prepare

The summer of 2014 was like all the other summers I cried upon returning back to school. However, this year was different my family was in immediate distress and something had to give. The boys were both in middle school and Keion was a Junior. The promise was to finish strong and attempt to repair our marriage all in one I'm your ride or die for REAL, failure was not an option. I expect everyone of my children to produce their best life. They would have no excuses! The boys would be attending private school 40 mins away from the house. So I came out of the classroom to drive my boys to and from school and I worked in between those hours.

One thing that I have learned about myself, is that once I make a decision to move, I'm out. It may take a moment, however, there is no turning back. Too focused on my next move. And when you're in God's will, doors just open. By the end of August I located an office space. By the end of September it was painted, carpeted, furnished, and ready to go! Attended training in New York the end of September and I was teaching class the first week in October. But God! When God moves, mountains fall. Nothing in my career ever moved so smooth.

This is when I learned the difference between my purpose and his purpose. Your gift will make room for you! Dimension is open and I could not feel more connected to God at this point. However, at the same time my marriage and my children were struggling. I saw the D word written on the wall and began to prepare for how I would support myself when the children were out of school. It was never my intention to leave before the kids went off to college. Everything was moving so quickly.

January I was on the Radio once a month til June. The name was building, and career wise I could not feel more closer to God! July we take our annual track vacation to Florida. I did my hair, looked good on the outside, he just kept looking at me like there she is. Yea, it was me on the inside but on the inside I was broken into little pieces just trying to hold on til my sentence was up. We each slept in separate rooms, I did not understand why he came back, it was worse emotionally. I could count how many times we went out alone. I tried to make Sunday our date night after class. It was good for a moment. Then one day he came into the house and said, words to me that I still don't understand. "You keep being disrespectful" and other things were stated. I was left confused and speechless. He did not come home that night. That was it for me, I had nothing left to fight for or with. I declared, announced it, I was done!

All this time I had been asking God to heal, restore, reconcile my family. However, it was clear at this time he was doing a new thing. And if I wanted to come there would be a process of refining that would be necessary. You can't go stressed out and be of service to anybody. For the next year, I would sleep, heal, and cry. I did not talk to any of my friends on a regular basis. I was rarely seen out, I could barely get out the bed, and I don't know the last time I took a bath…. Lol.. I know, I know, but I was healing. I remember reading the serenity prayer in my laundry room " God Grant me the Serenity to accept the things I cannot change, courage to change the things I can. And the wisdom to know the difference. It was not what I wanted for my family. But there would never be any true change without acknowledgment and accountability. So, now I'm here with Dimension APC, and healing Her Heart. I'm thankful for the Lord keeping me present for the three loves of my life: Keion, Donavon, and Jordan. Each day I get a little bit stronger, but everyday I wake up to peace of mind. For that I am Grateful!

No Fairytales

I remember leaving my lawyers office crying. The rose petal glasses were off and I realized all the lies and reality of what my marriage really consisted of. All I know is that I wanted the real thing or nothing at ALL! But the reality is a lot of marriages are business deals and you bargain for what's most important. Even with me now understanding this I still sought a Divorce because my desire was to be loved. Not for you to create what you wanted from a woman, I wanted to be loved for the beautiful woman that I am. That would be loving the Lord, caring for my family, and I find cleaning therapeutic.

I'm a women, a women with at heart! If you see me in pain, you don't just walk through me or act as though you have caused me no pain. Her Heart is fragile, gentle, and kind. It's endured a-lot, but each day she rises not to be inflicted with unnecessary caox or pain. From now on she guards Her Heart from which the lord dwells. Realistic about friendships, love, relationships, and family. Can't nobody do you like JESUS! For he loved me inspite of me.

I've listen to some of my girlfriends and they express how they missed the bullet, Be gentle but grateful. Because I was asked to walk through this battle and I have those moments of despair when I ask why? And then I get the reply of, why Not you! One never knows how success will change you.. So stop, your kids are still young, or they are grown and you will have grandchildren. Instead, praise God that he did not see fit to allow any of these things to happen to you. But also begin to pray for your future descendants that they shall also be spared for the light has nothing to do with darkness. God causes it to rain on the just and the unjust. (Mathew 5:45)

Her Heart pulls me all the way back to when I was twenty five. I read the insert in my "Women thou ought loose" bible which I loved. Thank you, Marshall Greenhow. It explained how God loved and judged Sarah and Rahab the same based on their heart. I had a very hard time understanding this at twenty five. I NOW understand that no matter what you do God loves us all the same. When you repent, it's symbolic of the rain being washed away by the windshield wiper, and that rain fall is never to be seen again. We continue to run our sins through our minds and allow others to hold us to judgement. And because of my lack of understanding and compassion. "It was good that I was afflicted", I'm humbled by others Hearts, and I'm so thankful that my Lord judges us by our heart.

Her Heart should be enough to wake you up to never lose her. Those vows are meant to be forever! However, when you disregard her distance, tears, fears, you have just disregarded Her Heart. Marriage is a partnership, a business deal as my stepfather explained. If you have two people working on one life, of course that one life will prosper and flourish. You never know what another person will do when power and money come into play. You never know how the other will handle prosperity and success until you see it with your eyes. Everyone is provided one life and at the end you will stand before God and will answer why you did not do as instructed. Exhausting oneself for my children and husband will not be sufficient. Then when I watched everyone and I mean everyone forsake me, after every sacrifice, I stood in amazement. But God! It was then that I understood If I did as instructed and put God first, those same folks would fall in place or it wouldn't even matter. Don't try to be God to your family was the lesson. You put God first and he will handle the consequences. See the offense was on me, the insult was on me. And I knew better. If you close your nostrils and hold your breathe you will eventually pass out. Well when you put yourself last and never fulfill your purpose on this earth you will expire. Women lose their minds everyday when that same person disappoints, betrays or leaves you. Why, because you closed your nostrils and your mouth. I'm not saying to forsake your family. I'm just explaining what happens when proper order and boundaries are not implemented and balance is not honored or displayed. Fulfilling your mates goals, dreams, and life purpose, is a two way street. No one should want you to hold your breath, Instead while working the other should clean while one cooks the other puts the kids in the bed. You must preserve each other's life, health, and energy. Everyone has a season you may stay home while the children are younger and then work when they reach a certain age. Ladies work from home or during school hours. Do something to bring goods to the store house. Education that can be used later, do something for you. And true men acknowledge the work and are grateful. I don't care if she is only bringing in $1. That $1 can turn into one million with the right love and support. Don't allow the enemy to make you think there is greater!

As my ex-husband visits our home with a clear vision I hear, " Wow what a beautiful home. Nothing changed, when he walks in and sees my hair done his eyes bulk up, like that's Kisha." The kids are almost grown leaving and we should be enjoying the fruits of our labor. Love does not always conquer all. I spent the first 20 years of my adult life praying,hoping,wishing, and loving my marriage and my family. The second half Kisha will spend putting God first and loving Kisha. Being kind and gentle to myself. When a woman snatches her life, her bag of goods, her love and walks away, that's a wrap! One can disregard the truth all you want, and act like you have done nothing! And I no longer need you to say I'm sorry. I did you wrong, you deserve better. It's ok, I forgive you! But listen, " Ain't it funny how love walks out and pain walks in. Because you are too far gone to back it up now! Skeleton's come out of the closet and chase you all around the room. Memories stand around like a Ghost, dance around in a sad slow tune. Just remember I gave it a long fight. " It's been to long!"

- *if you think you lonely now...... Bobby Womack*

Love Kisha

My Greatest Gift to You (My Mom)

My mother mailed me a package of letters three years prior to my liberation. I Read it when she mailed it however, it provided very little understanding at that time. As I "Little by Little" came to myself I remembered the letters that said, save this. And the moment I got home I read them and It was another piece of the puzzle that let me know my mom is an Award Winning Actress and she was working on my behalf contrary to what I believed. Wow!!!! Please remember that As I'm writing this book I still have very little understanding as to what is Really going on. But the most important thing is that I provide hope for my mind's strength. I'm assuming she is referencing a book because she listed pages…

Sent 04/11/2014

My greatest gift to you

Here are some of my notes and lessons going through life storms, notes to strengthen your faith; Share with your children now and then. Save this…..

Thank you Jesus

Regina

Mathew 1:18

The birth of Jesus Christ was on this wise:When as his mother Mary was to wed Joseph, before they came together, she was found with child of the Holy Ghost.

Joseph her Husband being a just man, and not willing to make her a public example. Was minded to put her away privately.

While he thought of these things. The angel of the Lord appeared unto him. In a dream, saying Joseph thou son of David, fear not to take unto thee Mary as thy wife: for that which is conceived in her is of the Holy Ghost.

Pg. 57

Be careful what you are hearing. The measure of thoughts and study you give will be the measure. That comes back to you.. Mark 4:24

Meditate on the word. Blessed is the man who walks and lives not in the counsel of the ungodly, nor stand in the path where sinners walk, nor sits down where the scornful gather... But his delight and desire are in the law of the Lord and on his law. He habitually meditates by day by night.

A.) According to webster

Meditate- mean 1,)

(This open letter is no longer able to be found)

I'M A SLAVE

I thought I was done with the book, however, I was encouraged by my aunt to continue. And after learning a few more details, I was sure that I had more to write. So her I am, writing more.

Words will never express the way that I felt when I learned that I AM A SLAVE. I went to a dark place, I was listening to scarface, Tupac, Dr. Dre. Your girl went Gangsta! Lol

How could this happen to me, I only wanted the best for everyone, and I never willing brought harm to anyone. I worked so hard to one day run for a political position, how could I BE A SLAVE. Everything that my father stated was no longer sounding crazy, it was all making sense. I googled my questions and found others who had made videos. The name was Targeted Individuals and the reality is that once put in the system, you could not be taken out. It involved the CIA, and it was highly organized. They had been watching my movement for years, I could recall it back ten years. They watch your movement and will then after five years of learning what you eat, who your friends and family are, learning where you go, the restaurants you eat, follow what products you use. Then they fall in for the kill to take you out! I was lost emotionally, and once I had my moment. I accepted the challenge and

Learned what I needed to do to survive, because my father said, "I shall not die".

The question still remained, who did this and why would they do this? My mind had to remain hopeful, so I could not focus on the who and the why. Because no one was talking and I mean nobody! That was the craziest part of it all. It's important to view non emotional people and to only view for a time, it is not a place to rest. Get in and get info. And get on preparing your survival is the key.

My pastor whom I call "The Good Shepherd" JH. Provided spiritual guidance with never meeting with me and speaking no more than five sentences to each other. He was praying for me and he was able to meet my needs by speaking to God on my behalf. And I am forever Grateful!!! Love you,

Pastor Hayes may every thing you touch be blessed.

I will tell every Pastor, stop draining yourself with trying to be God. Teach your congregation how to fish. What Do I mean, encourage them to pray for themselves, encourage them to lay hands on themselves, encourage them to go to war on behalf of their marriage and family, they are ultimately the captains of their ship. The storm highented towards the end of the summer of 2017. I was in class, by this time I'm aware of the devices to place a substance in my drinks by my students and the air control in my office was being manipulated by someone. I no longer kept food in my refrigerator, I carried a bag and it had everything I needed from toothpaste, soap, lotion, to my meals for the day. I even had to watch the presence of my children. Everyone close to me was a target. So, its my final class of the summer, and before we conclude my students wants to explain a book he was reading. I by now know to watch what I say and what I hear. The story depicts the major his son and a beautiful girl. He goes on and on even as I ask him to stop and try to speak over him. He then says that the goal is to kill the beautiful woman, and from their I blank out. My other student attempts to enforce positive response and I'm not understanding what is going on. I pack up to go home and I drive to the kids location which is at their dads. I was frozen to say the least. Everyone is acting funny so Im convinced that they had something to do with it. But why? It was all to much, and I had no one who could answer my questions. No one! I make it home, and I remain in the bed til Sunday. Unable to get out of bed to attend my present church Abner Baptist Church, Glen Allen. I go online to livestream 1st Baptist South Richmond. And I can tell they knew I was present, they sung and I sung along with the little strength that I had. That Wednesday I went to Bible study but it was canceled the first week and the next week Pastor was not present. I went because I need him to answer a question, and two inform him of my next step. The ride down 33 was interesting, it was something really unsettling about the whole storm. I felt unsafe so that next Sunday I listened on live stream again to First Baptist South Richmond and I attended sacred hour that evening. It was God giving me the strength to make this move, it definitely was not me. However, When I saw the Pastor's face Derik Jones, he had to fight back tears. I knew I had made the right decision. I just closed my eyes, Derik and I had attended college together. The senior Pastor is Dwight Jones, the former Mayor of

Richmond, Va. The experience was amazing and I knew I would join, that next Sunday. I attended the 9"15a.m. service and yes, I joined. That was a faith move it did not make sense to me or anyone else and I did not care. Im feeding the homeless, getting the right hand in fellowship working in the Cafe, I'm a member. The people are professional, loving, and taught me so much just by watching them handling service. I'm sure a lot of this was in part of their leader being in politics.

I'm starting to understand a few things that were keys early on. I know that Derik was fighting for me and I can see that he had come under attack. And words will never express how appreciative I am. My code to the universe was presenting itself in my life, never underestimate the power of your words and actions. It's the Love and Hip Hop Jerusalem "Notebook" at its best, Boom…..

Ok, before I forget the summer of June 17th I took Keion on a Boat trip to celebrate her first year in college. Now, sometime before we leave I'm getting an oil change. During this time I have my phone on and a couple who is also waiting says. You will go international June 17th. So, stay relevant. I'm not sure what this mean but I will say June 17, 2017 was the day our ship to Virgin Islands and Bahamas sailed. Guess what, they were also on the ship. People were very interesting on the ship, it was here that I learned that I was free. Later to learn that they had appealed the process. That set me back emotionally, it was devastating. I ate at the Savor for breakfast and something was in my cream cheese. I sat out in the Sun and drank all the water that I could. People on the ship took pictures and walked the ship holding up cups and shirts to indicate where we were. It was all very interesting, It was then that I understood what the international piece meant. What in the world is going on, I asked myself But still no reply was given. Upon my return I could see in the boys eyes that they had watched it all. Unable to show any emotions towards me they had to keep a blank face. See because in order for this all to work It has to all be made up in my mind. But, the devil is a liar.

WHERE DO I GO FROM HERE?

I had to learn how to love myself and how to know that I deserved so much more than I was allowing myself to enjoy. But God, he knew that I deserved so much more. And snatched me up, and for this I'm grateful. You never know who is watching you and who has the power to bless you.

I know longer see the world the same. I now understand how important each of our assignments are. Someone's life changing moment is depending on you being in position.. Pay attention to the people around you and listen to God's instruction. God just may need you to be someone's angel… My heart was broken, however, it was healed the moment I found Jesus. Who then placed me in my purpose to love and encourage others who may be broken and lost…

Taking it day by day and remaining patient with myself is a process. A process of progress not perfection and not making idols out of people. And remaining in love with Jesus every single day. Life is hard with Jesus, I don't want to know what it feels like without him. Two well known celebrities took their lives this week and it makes you think of that moment you wanted to let go. But God! You held on because we are taught that suffering does not last all ways. And that joy comes in the morning time. Having people surround you that cover and protect you in the good and the bad is a blessing! And I thank God for you.

So, Where do we go from here. We have already established that Im a beast! Just kidding. For Real where do I see my relationship with my kids, my business, my ministry, and will I just have friends or will I court? Great questions right? First, my relationship with my children are a soft spot. I love them with all my heart but no longer making an idol out of them. Keeping them in there appropriate place, between me and Jesus. I'll work hard at all of the above and give you all I got, however, you will have your appropriate place, between me and Jesus. I'll put no one before him, why? Because we serve a jealous God. And when I look back over my life God has had this same expectation all my life. I did not totally understand the accountability and the responsibility. Ok, let's stay focused, where do we go from here? Well let me explain how God has prepared me for my knew life. I was isolated from family and friends. All that I could do was depend on God as my source, he was all I had and I learned all I needed.. I could call him at 3am and he would answer, every time. During this time I got to know who I really was and what my purpose was in life. I had little to know money and I was depending on God to raise me up from the bottom. Ok, let me tell you, I had to battle those who knew I was tithing but not having enough to pay all of my bills. Tithing is one of my bills matter of fact its my first bill. I was on my back and I did not know how I was going to get up let alone how I was going to make a dollar. I learned that when I got up it was God who got me up not I, my momma, not my kids, But God. So, me tithing became my thank you Lord and I prayed that he continued to get me out of bed. If I made $500 I was giving $50 dollars, if I made a $1000 I was giving a $100. The devil wants to distract your mind with fleshly thoughts, Pastor is driving a NEW Bens, girl

Pastor is tithing. Girl sister so and so just brought a new house, girl she is tithing too. It's the secret. The test will be for me to tithe when that million dollar check comes in for Dimension and Her Heart. I'll write that $100,000 Check as well, it's the secret. What's going to happen when Boo Boo comes (AKA BOAZ), Boaz is in for a big kiss and the ride of his life. (hum, maybe I should reword that) See he has to keep me safe and I have to keep him wild. He shall also be between Jesus and I. I still believe in love, I just now believe in Happily Ever After!

Test Like A Champ

I'm not one to play the victim…. And I never want to be the person that says I did not deserve that. Because if the truth be told, sometimes bad things happen to good people. It rains on the just and the unjust. However, our God promises to work it out for your good, and HE did. I now have a testimony with my test so" it is good for me that I was afflicted." (Psalm 119:71) Today I was so weary that I took my blanket and wrapped myself up in our theatre chairs, as I just prayed to the lord that he would rock me to sleep in his arms. I remember feeling a warmth come over my body and I just cried and fell to sleep. In the back of my mind I was thinking is this what serving my father feels like. What the Devil meant for bad, God turned it around and used it for his good. Why was I weary, when you're in battle you will become weary but you must not faint. Instead I would rather "take it like a champ" (New Birth, Bishop Kenneth Mooire) and move forward. This does not mean in my alone time that I don't moan, groan, or cry out to God! Because I do. I give myself that moment then I dry my eyes. And with my eyes wide open, I get back to work. Because I'm committed to being that women to press forward with a smile and of great cheer! Devil you took your best shot. I stumbled, tripped, fell, hell I even passed out. Still I rise, and to God be the Glory, for my father in heaven wishes to put me back together again. I'm reminded of Joseph whose brothers threw him in the pit, because he was his father's favorite. Joseph pleaded with his brother's, as a merchant was passing, and they sold him into slavery. Joseph rose to work for a prominent figure but was once again discarded. He was throne in jail over accusations that he has sexually assaulted the man's wife. But God! Joseph was then called on by the highest authority of the land and in within this position had full control of the land. Joseph persisted with Excellence in-spite of. No it's not right and no it's not fair but get back to work! The land needs you, so shake it off!!!

Boaz and Ruth

Maybe you have yet to Read the book of Ruth, well after this chapter you will pull it out and read it for yourself. Boaz is the international name you hear from women in waiting,

"I'm waiting on my Boaz". When you read this chapter you will know that it is our job to work and in doing so our husbands will see us shining. Shining in the fields that they own. Girl, I'm telling you what I know, It happend to me and for me. I was working from sun up to sun down and had no idea that I was in his field. As I look back over the sequence of events. I remembered a consistent pattern of students coming to my office after I did my monthly radio lesson. It turned out to be a hit with the community and the Numbers at the Radio station showed that they liked it (I was in his field). My students were somehow always connected to the Mayor or First Baptist. I now know the radio station Loved him,(I was in his field) my students he sent me, I still don't know how till this day(I was in his field). My Naomi I believe was the Assistant to the Delegate whose office was directly in front of mine. Yes, that business I stepped out on faith to start(I was in his field). Ok, The Book of Ruth in the bible is now one of my favorite books. Ladies if my book "Her Heart" does nothing else for you, but express why you wait on your man and woman of God. This man of God whom I had been in his fields, was yet the same man God had told me would be my husband over 20 years ago. I'm amazed and often in disbelieve that the God I serve saw fit to give me a second chance. Ya'll I was working in his field and I did not even know. He was watching me and taking notes and I did not even know. I was working thinking I was doing something and the whole time he had his men throwing blessings in my path just for me. He never spoke to me he never interacted with me in private. Ya'll he showed me so much respect, favor and honor he loved me even when I did not love myself. I was broke and broken and yet he still said, "I want that one". If I could tell the truth I never thought God would give me an opportunity to be with him. However, every man that I met and fell for demonstrated his character and qualities almost to a T. I'm so humbled and feeling emotionally blessed that he answered God's cry to rescue me and All I can say is he won't be sorry! For God has truly favored me in the midst of my mess. "I love me some him." What happens from here, I have know Idea but I do know that God Got it! Job 8:7 though your beginning was small, yet your latter end would greatly increase.

THE
BEGINNING

Go Get Your Life Back!
(31 days of Prayer)

My mind healed and my situation changed when I learned to call on the throne and not the phone. So, for the next 31 days, yes 31 days. We will become our very own prayer Warriors. Snatch back Your mind, your dreams, your eating habits, healthy thoughts. Before we can be of service to anyone, we must first serve ourselves. Something may have you down but you are not out. NOW, snatch back your mind,marriage,career, health, relationships, whatever the case maybe let's take it by FORCE.

Materials needed::

1. **Your very own** Her Heart **Book**
2. **Log on to facebook and friend request Her Heart chat room**
3. **Get your bible**
4. **Pen or Pencil**
5. **Designated room, closet,**
6. **Commit to 5am prayer live with me**

DAY 1

Scripture : (Jeremiah 32:17)
O Sovereign Lord! You have made the heavens and earth by your great power. Nothing is too hard for you!!!

Prayer list :

_____

_____

_____

_____

_____

_____

Prayer :

_____

_____

_____

_____

_____

_____

DAY 2

Scripture :(Proverbs 4:23)
Above all else guard your heart for everything you do flows from it...

Prayer list :

_____

_____

_____

_____

_____

_____

Prayer :

_____

_____

_____

_____

_____

_____

DAY 3

Scripture :(Psalm 103:2)
Let all that I am praise the Lord ; may I never forget the good things he does for me.

Prayer list :

_____

_____

_____

_____

_____

_____

Prayer :

_____

_____

_____

_____

_____

_____

DAY 4

Scripture :(Psalm 91:4)
He will cover you with his feathers and his faithfulness, will be your shield..

Prayer list :

_____

_____

_____

_____

_____

_____

Prayer :

_____

_____

_____

_____

_____

_____

DAY 5

Scripture : (Psalm 51:10)

Create in me a pure heart, O God and renew a steadfast spirit within me...

Prayer list :

_____

_____

_____

_____

_____

_____

Prayer :

_____

_____

_____

_____

_____

_____

 DAY 6

Scripture : (Isiah 41:10)

Don't be afraid for I am with you. Do not be dismayed, For I am your God. I will strengthen you. I will help you, I will uphold you with my victorious right hand.

Prayer list :

_____

_____

_____

_____

_____

_____

Prayer :

_____

_____

_____

_____

_____

_____

 DAY 7

Scripture : (Romans 12:2)
Don't copy the behavior and customs of this world, but let God transform you into a new person by changing the way you think. Then you will know what God wants you to do. And you will know how good and pleasing and perfect his will really is.

Prayer list :

_____
_____
_____
_____
_____
_____

Prayer :

_____
_____
_____
_____
_____
_____

# DAY 8

Scripture :(Psalm 62:5)
He alone is my rock and my salvation, my fortress where I will never be shaken.

Prayer list :

_____

_____

_____

_____

_____

_____

Prayer :

_____

_____

_____

_____

_____

_____

DAY 9

Scripture : (Luke 1:45)
"You are blessed, because you believed that the Lord would do what he said."

Prayer list :

_____

_____

_____

_____

_____

_____

Prayer :

_____

_____

_____

_____

_____

_____

 DAY 10

Scripture:: (Isiah 43)
But now, O Isreal, the Lord who created you says.
Do not be afraid, for I have ransomed you.

Prayer list :

_____

_____

_____

_____

_____

_____

Prayer :

_____

_____

_____

_____

_____

_____

 DAY 11

Scripture :(Luke 22:49)
Not my will but yours be done.

Prayer list :

_____

_____

_____

_____

_____

_____

Prayer :

_____

_____

_____

_____

_____

_____

 DAY 12

Scripture :(Malachi 3:6)
For I am the Lord I changeth not.

Prayer list :

_____
_____
_____
_____
_____
_____

Prayer :

_____
_____
_____
_____
_____
_____

 DAY 13

Scripture : (Job 1:12)
"Do whatever you want with everything he possesses, but don't harm him physically."

Prayer list :

_____
_____
_____
_____
_____
_____

Prayer :

_____
_____
_____
_____
_____
_____

 DAY 14

Scripture : (Psalm 7:17)
I will thank the Lord because he is just; I will sing praise to the name of the Lord most high.

Prayer list :

_____

_____

_____

_____

_____

_____

Prayer :

_____

_____

_____

_____

_____

_____

 DAY 15

Scripture : (Jonah 1:9)
"I worship the LOrd, the God of heaven, who made the sea and the land."

Prayer list :

_____

_____

_____

_____

_____

_____

Prayer :

_____

_____

_____

_____

_____

_____

# DAY 16

Scripture : (John 3:16)
"For God so loved the world that he gave his only son, so that everyone who believes in him will not perish but have eternal life."

Prayer list :

_____

_____

_____

_____

_____

_____

Prayer :

_____

_____

_____

_____

_____

_____

 DAY 17

Scripture : (Mathew 17:20)
"You didn't have enough faith jesus told him."
I assure you, even if you has faith as small as a
mustard seed you could say to this mountain,
move from here to there, "and it would move.
Nothing would be impossible."

Prayer list :

_____
_____
_____
_____
_____
_____

Prayer :

_____
_____
_____
_____
_____
_____

DAY 18

Scripture : (2 Chronicles 20 : 15)
Do not be afraid! Don't be discouraged by this mighty army for the battle is not yours, but God's.

Prayer list :

_____
_____
_____
_____
_____
_____

Prayer :

_____
_____
_____
_____
_____
_____

 DAY 19

Scripture : (Luke 6:45)
"Whatever is in your heart determines what you say."

Prayer list :

_____

_____

_____

_____

_____

_____

Prayer :

_____

_____

_____

_____

_____

_____

DAY 20

Scripture :(Psalm 16:8)
"I know the Lord is always with me. I will not be shaken for he is right beside me."

Prayer list :

_____

_____

_____

_____

_____

_____

Prayer :

_____

_____

_____

_____

_____

_____

 DAY 21

Scripture : (Psalm 30:5)
Weeping may go on all night, but joy comes with the morning.

Prayer list :

_____
_____
_____
_____
_____
_____

Prayer :

_____
_____
_____
_____
_____
_____

DAY 22

Scripture : (2 Chronicles 20:21)
"Give thank to the Lord ; his faithful love endures forever!"

Prayer list :

_____

_____

_____

_____

_____

_____

Prayer :

_____

_____

_____

_____

_____

_____

DAY 23

Scripture :(Isiah 40 : 3-5)
Make a straight smooth road through the desert for our God. Fill the valleys and level the hills. Straighten out the curves and smooth off the rough spots.

Prayer list :

_____

_____

_____

_____

_____

_____

Prayer :

_____

_____

_____

_____

_____

_____

 DAY 24

Scripture (Job 33 :15)
He speaks in dreams, in visions of the night when
deep sleep falls on people as they lie in bed.

Prayer list :

_____

_____

_____

_____

_____

_____

Prayer :

_____

_____

_____

_____

_____

_____

DAY 25

Scripture : (Psalm 27:5)
For hr will conceal me there when troubles come. He will hide me in his snactuary. He will place me out of reach on a high rock. Then I will my head high. Above my enemies who surround me, At his tabernacle I will offer sacrifices with shout of joy.

Prayer list :

_____
_____
_____
_____
_____
_____

Prayer :

_____
_____
_____
_____
_____
_____

DAY 26

Scripture : (John 10 :27)
My sheep listen to my voice ; I know them, and they follow me.

Prayer list :

_____
_____
_____
_____
_____
_____

Prayer :

_____
_____
_____
_____
_____
_____

 Day 27

Scripture : (Isiah 40 : 29-31)

He gives power to those who are tired and worn out. He offers strength to the week. Even youths will become exhausted, and young men will give up. But those who wait on the Lord will find new strength. They will fly high on wings like eagles. They will Run and not grow weary. They will walk and not faint.

Prayer list :

_____

_____

_____

_____

_____

_____

Prayer :

_____

_____

_____

_____

_____

_____

 DAY 28

Scripture : (Samuel 10 :18)
And he gave them this message from the Lord,
the God of Israel: I brought you from Egypt and
rescued you from the Egyptians and from all of
the nations that were oppressing you.

Prayer list :

_____

_____

_____

_____

_____

_____

Prayer :

_____

_____

_____

_____

_____

_____

 DAY 29

Scripture : (Peter 5:7)
Give all your worries and cares to God, for he cares about what happens to you.

Prayer list :

_____

_____

_____

_____

_____

_____

Prayer :

_____

_____

_____

_____

_____

_____

 DAY 30

Scripture :(2 Corinthians 5 :17)
What this means is that those who become Christians become new persons. They are not the same anymore, for the old life is gone. A new life has begun!

Prayer list :

_____

_____

_____

_____

_____

_____

Prayer :

_____

_____

_____

_____

_____

_____

 DAY 31

Words will never describe the despair I felt when I learned of my circumstance. I never knew such a dark world even existed. But God! My protector, my healer, my confidant, my lover, my friend, my doctor, my lawyer,my provider. My God rocked me to sleep that night and all I felt was a warm sense of peace come over me. Things always get worse before they get better. Within my isolation the devil whispered, "nobody cares, you're not going to make it out, no one loves you let alone likes you. And I remember being in the shower crying to God. Like I had done so many times "Lord Please help" I can't do this all by myself. I played music all day long, I listened to youtube preaching of Paula White in the beginning. I went to sleep listening to Charles Stanley. And I wrapped it up with T.D. Jakes.. My soul was anchored in the Lord. But those last 30 days I knew would be the darkest hour. So, being proactive to sustain my strength mentally and spiritually I began 5a.m. prayer every morning Monday - Friday. I had bible lessons on Wednesdays, and Happy Hour on Friday. Each was necessary to draw me closer to God and to provide hope. The final hour before day break is always the darkest hour. And that Sunday, I cried all the way to church. I was scared to get excited for the battle was real! And Tuesday the 29th was the longest day of my life. I kept myself busy all day active and engaged. And now it's 9:17p.m.(August 29th) and I want to tell you the ten lessons my journey has taught me.

10. Psalm 120 :1	In my trouble I cried to the Lord, and he answered me.
9. Jeremiah 29:11	For I know the plans I have to prosper you and not harm you, declares the Lord. Plans to give you hope and a future.
8. Romans 8:31	If God is for us, who can Be against us.
7. 2 Chronicles 20:15	Do not fear or be dismayed because of this great multitude. For the battle is not yours but God's.

6. Phillippians 4:13   I can do all things
                        through Christ, who
                        strengthens me.

5. Isiah 54:17   No weapon formed
                        against you shall
                        Prosper.

4. Psalm 91:11   For he will give
                        his angels charge
                        concerning you, in all
                        your ways.

3. Luke 12:48   For unto whom so ever
                        much is given of him
                        shall be much required.

2. John 8:36   If the son sets you free,
                        you are free indeed.

1. Psalm 119:71   It was good for me to be
                        afflicted. So that I might
                        learn your Decrees.

It was then that I praised God in my circumstance. It was then that I learned to patiently wait on the Lord. It was then that I became a warrior instead of a worrier. It was then that I learned in my weakness he is strong. It was here that I learned that God was just as much in love with me as I was with him. It was then that he told me step back, I Got this!!!